Advance Praise for The

"At a time when so many of our la [...] into deepening dysfunction, Milenko Matanovic brings his decades of wise and creative experience to bear in an inspiring and highly readable handbook for the kind of democracy we can all practice."
—*Daniel Kemmis, former mayor of Missoula, Montana, speaker and minority leader of the Montana House of Representatives, and author of Community and the Politics of Place*

"Combining terrific personal stories and easy-to-follow skills outlines, Matanovic has written an extremely useful handbook for engaged residents and local government leaders alike. To rebuild the trust between the public and our governing institutions demands understanding the hard trade-offs inherent in many local policy decisions, and this guide provides invaluable instruction on how to improve our public meetings."
—*Pete Peterson, Dean & Sr. Fellow, Pepperdine School of Public Policy*

"The most powerful form of community involvement starts with the expression of respect and understanding. It is followed by the creation and nurturing of trusting relationships. This is not easy. Trust must be earned. Milenko Matanovic gives us the gift of his years of experience and his approach to civic participation that leads us to a deeper understanding of what it means to call ourselves an active member of a community."
—*Mark Okazaki, Executive Director, Neighborhood House – Seattle, WA*

"Many years ago, I saw this quote on the wall of a school in Columbus, Ohio, and I retained it through the years: Education and Morality constitute the Majesty and Force of Free Government. It describes the attributes of a great society. Milenko's booklet is an inspired and intelligent tool for its pursuit."
—*Elliott Gould, actor*

"Milenko Matanovic blends the political with the deeply personal is his latest work, the culmination of a career devoted to envisioning a better way and then empowering that vision in the hands of his countrymen, neighbors, and the communities he serves. 'Everyday Democracy' is essential for balancing inclusiveness and decisiveness, the organizer's two primary building blocks to success, and a challenge that only the likes of Matanovic can tackle."
—*Ian Martinez, UpZones podcast*

"We evaluate societies by how individuals accept others. Are others an obstacle against my personal wellbeing or do we create common wellbeing? In the first case, we create a society of alienated individuals, great inequality and poverty, unhappy citizens and lots of criminal activities. In the second case, people cooperate across differences, they fragment less, and experience higher satisfaction where everyone can contribute according to their ability and knowledge. Because contributions are welcome, people are more likely to be engaged. This small booklet with big ideas offers excellent examples of how we can improve our society and increase people's happiness."
—*Matjaž Hanžek, Steward for Human Rights, Slovenia*

"In New Zealand we have been brutally reminded of the danger of our communities being separated in bubbles of like-minded people. Bringing people with diverse ideas together and helping them shape a shared vision takes skill and talent, but is so important. Milenko has generously shared 30 years of practice in 'fierce facilitation' which provides us with principles and tools to grow a better future - meeting by meeting. We value the experience of the Pomegranate Centre and will encourage staff to make use of this great resource."
—*Karen Johns, Specialist Advisor, Auckland Council*

"Like its author, this handbook is insightful, wise, provocative, and practical. If even a small fraction of public meetings were to apply the principles described in these pages, the ripple effects in civic life would be tremendous: dysfunction would turn into creation, resentment into responsibility, helplessness into power. Read Milenko's book and put it to use."
—*Eric Liu, CEO of Citizen University and author of You're More Powerful Than You Think: A Citizen's Guide to Making Change Happen*

"At a time when communication seems to value shouting rather than listening, inflexibility rather than respect, it's refreshing to see a blueprint for civic engagement that encourages everyone to speak up and everyone to listen. In this short but profound essay, Milenko provides coaching for citizens and community leaders alike that can transform input into meaningful action. A must-read for anyone involved in local government."
—*Representative Kate Webb, Vermont House of Representatives, Chair, House Education Committee*

"In clear, lucid writing Milenko draws on thirty years of work with scores of organizations and communities to establish bonds of trust and understanding- all to weave individuals into groups and community. This powerful cogent piece shows the positive effects of social capital; the ways that people in relationships can reach goals that would have been far beyond the grasp of individuals in isolation."
— *Lewis Feldstein, Co-Chair of The Saguaro Seminar, co-author with Robert Putman of 'Better Together.'*

"As a lifelong community activist, I have sat through hundreds of civic and volunteer meetings -- many successful, many not -- and all would have benefited from Milenko's "ground rules for collaboration." Through simple but inspiring examples, he celebrates the many ways a potentially contentious meeting can become an example of "everyday democracy" in which everyone feels they had input and achieved something special, rather than simply winning or losing a battle. Anyone who bemoans the future of democracy need only look around your neighborhood: it starts close to home, with you. Use these guidelines to make your community a more functional but also beautiful place for all."
—*Deborah Szekely, U.S. Diplomat, Co-Founder of Rancho La Puerto and Founder of The Golden Door*

Turning Community Meetings into
Engines for Collaboration

The Case for Everyday Democracy

Milenko Matanovič

ISBN: 978-1-7330658-1-8

Table of Contents

Introduction

When Thomas Jefferson wrote America's Declaration of Independence, he set out two core principles that he held to be self-evident: That all people are created equal, and that they hold fundamental rights to life, liberty, and the pursuit of happiness.

In my 30 years leading the Pomegranate Center, I have engaged with communities around the world to help them build shared visions of a collaborative, constructive future. In that time, I have developed some principles of my own that I believe any community can utilize to promote what I call "everyday democracy"—the procedures and habits that we bring to our community deliberations.

This handbook distills those principles into a compact form for use by anyone, with a particular focus on how we can use public meetings to foster effective collaboration. Can we turn these existing meetings into more joyful learning experiences where we ask what can go right?

Before I dive in, however, let me spend a moment on the principles that, like Jefferson, I hold to be self-evident:

- That all people are essential, and that the future we build must be for all.

- That we will need to leave behind some old habits and form new relationship patterns.
- That when shaping our collective destiny, together we always know more.
- That collaboration—across differences that exist in our cities and towns—is square one for the future.
- That it only takes a few to derail collaboration. All of us will need to bring our best selves. forward as we walk into our shared future
- That community meetings are ready-made "classrooms" for learning new habits of being and thinking together.
- That in the world where everyone pushes their ideas, the new heroes will become those able to connect those ideas into larger patterns and shared discoveries.
- That how we talk with each is as important as what we say.

Collaborative Democracy in Action

A park on the edge of a low-income, very diverse neighborhood was in trouble. People were dealing drugs. Parents were afraid for their kids' safety, and the police had difficulty maintaining control because the dealers had many escape routes.

The community called Pomegranate Center to assist. We organized a meeting to hear ideas from community members for how to turn the space around so it would serve all and become safe.

"Bring people to that area. Many eyes will make it safer."

"Yes, let's build a promenade through that area."

"How wide should it be?" I asked.

"Wide enough for two couples to pass each other without needing to step off the path."

I took out a measuring tape. Two couples paused as they passed each other, and we measured the width of the path.

"It needs to be a bit wider for larger people," suggested

another. We added two feet to the original measurement.

"Family picnics," said the next person.

"A platform for music and dancing."

"Yes, and small hills for children to climb and explore."

"But not too high," said a mother. "I want to be able to always see them."

I asked her how high it should be. She moved her hand between her shoulder and waist until she found the right height. I measured and recorded it.

In less than two hours, we heard dozens of ideas. When I asked the group which ideas stood out, some naturally rose to the top. We held a design workshop to develop drawings and sketches. We conducted an open house to present the designs. People were thrilled and shared their desire to help with building.

Two months later, the same community members worked with us to build the dance floor and the promenade and the mounds and picnic tables. They rightly felt that they did it. It was their project. They succeeded in making the park safe for their families.

Collaborative democracy works like this. The sharp lines between those who decide and those impacted disappear. The lines between professionals and amateurs soften. Ordinary people know a lot. They can turn into designers. They are smart about how things should work in their lives. They know it in their bodies, and in their caring for their children.

To ignore this folk wisdom is not wise.

Part 1:
Why Collaborative Skills are Needed

When I immigrated to the United States in the 1970s, I discovered many a town with no center and was taken aback by places friendlier to cars than to people. The lack of central plazas and parks, so common in Europe, was jarring. I saw plenty of metaphors for individual, corporate, and government life: McMansions, skyscrapers, and highways. But where were the metaphors for the people and the connections between them? I must have decided then to become a community builder. I felt the need to connect with other people and ideas, to cultivate interdependence, and to use my skills to create bridges and forge interdisciplinary understanding. I felt that, as an artist, I could be most useful if I offered my ability to connect the dots between everyday life and creativity—something that came naturally to me.

After orienting myself to my new country, instead of pursuing my artistic career, I decided to "loan" my skills to others. I wanted to see if I could help people replace parking spaces with gathering places. In 1986, I founded the non-profit Pomegranate Center to engage community members in becoming more creative, productive, and joyful participants able to shape their future together.

I worked with communities, not for them. I helped others find their creativity. I focused on others feeling pride and ownership of the work. My focus was to design a process where they would know that they did it, not that anyone did it for them. This is, perhaps, where my artistic experience played out: the process and the end result were inseparable. So, if we were to create stronger communities, people living there must be involved not just as passive observers but as creators.

To succeed, my colleagues and I had to sharpen our facilitation skills. Our community projects provided an excellent laboratory to develop processes that included many voices and perspectives, that happened continuously so people could still remember the last meeting, that allowed for spontaneity and creativity, and could be done in a way that people felt ownership and satisfaction at every stage.

The key ingredients of the process were good communication with all the partners; thorough preparation and clarity to maximize each meeting's potential; neutral facilitators who fiercely protect the process so the participants can focus on the content; and a set of ground rules to nudge the participants to be constructive, collaborative, creative, and holistic in their thinking. We basically asked them to shift from thinking about what could go wrong to what could go right. This led to better ideas.

Over the next three decades, we developed the Pomegranate Method, refined by testing different approaches to community engagement and correcting failures. Now, we focus exclusively on training and mentoring, offering practical tools for individuals, groups, and agencies to work inclusively across multiple affinity groups. Our goal is to prepare individuals, organizations, and society for a collaborative future. We think that every community can significantly benefit by having a roster of fierce (I will say more about this later) and neutral facilitators available to assist governments, non-profits, and businesses with a process that exhibits integrity. Our process balances inclusiveness, where all are invited to shape the decision, with decisiveness wherein a short period, shared agreements and arrangements can be achieved.

Public Meetings are Where Things Happen

In the US we have developed formal procedures—elections—for selecting our representatives. This is politics.

In between those elections are smaller but significant events that shape the future of our communities, where local governments and private developers and non-profits reach out to communities to receive input and guidance. Hundreds, if not thousands, of such engagements occur every week across our states, cities, towns, and neighborhoods. What happens at these events, and how we choose to conduct ourselves where the common good is at stake, is the field of everyday democracy. It means participating at the local level in decisions and in the creation of institutions, places, and systems that inform our lives together.

I am sure that some meetings are engaging, creative, and productive, resulting in joyful learning and shared decisions. My experience tells me, however, that they are rare.

It was early in my Pomegranate work when I decided

to attend meetings mandated by the Washington State's Growth Management Act (GMA) of 1990 to figure out how to foster growth while containing sprawl, protecting the environment, promoting sustainable economic development, and increasing the quality of life for all. The Act's approach was to push the decision-making to the local level, encouraging each city and town to hold public meetings to get people involved in the critical conversations about how to balance growth and quality of life. I attended one such meeting with about 10 others. Half were property owners and developers; the other half were the "usual suspects" who, I was told, attended most council meetings. I was surprised to find out how cranky they were.

In my innocence, I expected ideas about the future. I anticipated innovation and excitement. After all, there was a great opportunity to shape the future with other citizens and with governments. But people at the meeting were mainly concerned with whether they would still be able to develop their properties, and what restrictions they would encounter. The "usual suspects" were complaining about the intrusion of government into their lives, and about taxes that would need to be raised to manage growth. And the fate of our community rested with these people? I left the meeting full of disappointment. I decided at that moment that there must be a better way to engage communities and that I would do something about it.

At a recent workshop in Seattle with a government agency and a non-profit organization, we asked for the participants to write on a whiteboard the challenging behaviors they witnessed at their community meetings. Here is the list of the most frequently mentioned habits:

17

- focus only on self
- speak softly, slowly and at great length; make incomprehensible statements
- refuse to follow the facilitator's guidance and reject the facilitator's qualifications
- speak forever; grandstand
- express negativity and anger, and resort to yelling
- shake their heads when others speak
- threaten legal action; threaten to withdraw
- cry and use tears as a weapon
- come with fixed agenda
- interrupt repeatedly
- won't let go and move on
- express a sense of entitlement
- exhibit overt racism
- remain unwilling to consider any new ideas
- see conspiracies

We've learned the hard way that each one of these challenging habits has the power to derail the process.

Seeing how easily the process can malfunction, we started to develop our own strategies and procedures. To expedite our learning, I observed many community engagement processes. We began to test different approaches in our projects and quickly learned what has the power to shift the meetings into collaborative, creative, and joyful events.

Square One: Wide Collaboration

The very word "collaboration" has a shadow meaning: collaborating with the enemy, for example. Submission, weakness, something for those who can't make it by themselves, therefore un-American. Or perhaps something that is nice to have, but not necessary in the long run.

Our practice has proven the opposite: Collaboration is square one for the future. The complexities of our world require all of us to learn to combine our insights and to consult rather than convince each other.

Broad collaboration reaches across our differences, professions, and sectors: private, public, and not-for-profit. Collaboration is second nature for actors and dancers and jazz musicians. Perhaps we can learn something from them.

Community collaboration is about discovery. It is gutsy work where we must always adjust to the ideas and impulses of others. It requires us to be willing to change, and this takes courage. It is not for those promoting themselves, their organizations, or fixed ideas. Collaboration thrives in the process of gradual discovery in which ideas from multiple sources join to create a solution more potent than any single point of view. When ideas resonate, the result is always "multiple victories," a piece of work that meets many separate goals. Then each participant can say, "I did this."

In collaboration, great ideas rise to the surface because they have value, not just because they have the most vocal promoters. I have seen this in many meetings. Sometimes the most significant insights come from the least expected sources: a child, a quiet writer, the mother of a two-year-old, or a scientist. From their unique view, they see possibilities that others cannot.

At first, offerings from unfamiliar territory seem like extraneous noise, easy to reject. They don't fit with our worldview. They arise from different understandings of the world and offer various benefits. Listening creates a learning atmosphere that helps us understand that others may see the same situation through a different set of priorities and values. We quickly discover that while we are great at some things, we are also blissfully ignorant of many other things. When we accept this, it naturally leads us to engage others who can compensate for our ignorance. We then ask questions: "What do you see? Tell us more." Collaboration rests on the ability to hear and take in the ideas of others and incorporate them into our plans.

Artistic Process and the Pomegranate Method

I have found that the artistic process is a useful framework for community work. The creative process is a cycle. New, original works start with silence, with listening and observing, until a compelling insight announces itself. The artist anchors the original idea through notes or sketches and prototypes. She chooses basic textures and patterns for the work, the best possible form for the work's intent. From then onward, the action shifts outward, toward expressing and crafting. Finally, the artists show or perform the new creation so it can be appreciated and bring new insights to the audience. The whole process, then, is an ecological cycle from an idea into reality, from intuition into form. Of course, artists sell their work to sustain themselves. But on a spiritual, emotional, and psychological level, the work needs to be let go of, released, to create space for new creations. Then the cycle is complete and can restart, leading to new, improved works.

•

Béla Fleck, banjo virtuoso and master improviser and musical collaborator, told me during a conversation, "The bottom line is that you must be willing to let others shine. When my attitude is simply that I want to play great, this is not as good as when I want everyone to be great."

•

Pomegranate Center uses a similar cyclical process, but the studio now is a community of people. Instead of making a journey alone, we do it together, using different experiences and insights to shape and guide the process. Once Pomegranate Center gets invited into a community, we spend time "wiring the project for success." It is the time to listen and learn. We do our best to understand the local conditions of culture, politics, and resources, as well as the project's site. We make sure that the project leaders understand the collaborative approach and that they will support it for the duration. We assemble a group of community leaders who provide local knowledge and help us engage with the community. We've learned that this preparatory work is absolutely essential, that if we make an inch of a mistake early on, the gap will be miles wide later. It is not unusual that this phase of the project takes almost as long as the visible and active part of the project.

Every project is a journey from ideas to technical solutions. Engagement is most meaningful at the beginning where we can imagine the project's essence. This is the "poetic" side of the project. It is about its purpose and meaning. At the beginning of the process, where the direction is being determined, organizers must be committed to hearing a broad spectrum of views. The beauty of the community is that people care about different things. Everyone should have a chance to express their ideas. I've done this with up to 200 people, and I am always thrilled to hear unexpected solutions that emerge from their collective wisdom.

The goal is to listen to all ideas and to move quickly, without judgment. The value of such a collective brainstorming exercise is that all participants begin to understand that the field of ideas is broad, that their particular view is one of many, and therefore, that the goal should be to find a way to serve many purposes, not just the ones dear to particular individuals.

Unless we ask for input, we should not call it engagement. There must be a question that the participants will be asked to answer. If there are no questions, there is no engagement. The more engaged people are, the more they have a chance to contribute and the more ownership of the project they will experience.

Too often, the organizers are reluctant to invite people into the project's early stages. This is a mistake. I attended a meeting where people were asked for input, only to be told at the end that the mayor and the council had already made critical decisions. "Watch me not come to the next meeting," I heard one participant state. To this individual, that meeting was a farce, a betrayal of his willingness to contribute to his community. Only a tiny percentage of people participate in town halls and community meetings. When people think their ideas will matter and then discover the opposite, this little slice gets even thinner. This is not good for democracy.

Respect Time

People have limited time to give to community meetings. If meetings are not organized and facilitated well, people will not return. Throughout this handbook I will emphasize the importance of the facilitator, who is central to managing time throughout the process.

The best community meetings I led never lasted more than two hours. And the best planning processes had three meetings in total. It is possible to do a fantastic amount of good work in a relatively short amount of time. Rapid progress is a pleasure; people return over and over when they can feel progress.

The goal is to replace the quantity of meetings with quality.

A successful meeting has a short welcome, a well-prepared and concise presentation that helps everyone understand the "whys" and "whats" of the project, a generous amount of time for people to offer their ideas and insights, and a closing statement on the next steps.

The meeting facilitators need to prepare well. The time before the meeting that wires the project for success correctly is critical. Meetings typically don't start precisely on time, so there is usually about one hour and fifty minutes of working time.

A respected local leader should open meetings. Their role is ceremonial. It is important for the facilitator to coach this leader to only welcome all the participants and introduce the facilitators. I learned the importance of this constraint when a mayor greeted the community and then launched into a 15-minute reelection speech, shrinking our working time to just 95 minutes.

The facilitator then takes the lead to clarify the goals of the project and the meeting, explain the agenda as well as roles and responsibilities: The participants' task is to offer insights; consultants and government staff should provide technical information if needed but otherwise should mostly listen; facilitators ensure that all participants engage and that the meeting stays on schedule.

The trickiest part is to craft the project background. I witnessed a meeting where the presentation was one hour long, with slide upon slide explaining a lot of technical details. Peoples' eyes glazed over. When the presenter turned to them for input, they did not know what they were supposed to add. The goal is to provide precise information in about 15 minutes and not overwhelm with details. This presentation should cover the funding and its restrictions; project timeline; the key players and their roles; what is possible and not possible; the site; information on the neighborhood and adjacent amenities; how community input will be used and integrated into the plan; examples of projects that successfully met similar goals; and what will happen after the meeting.

This is a lot of information to pack into a short time. It takes a lot of preparation to make it sing.

After the presentation, we usually organize a short

Q&A to clarify any remaining questions. Presenting the project background with clarity will send a signal that the organizers mean business and that people's ideas matter. Meeting attendees will notice such integrity and respond in kind, rewarding the meeting by offering constructive, creative, and future-oriented ideas.

Then we move to the input. We review the ground rules that focus on being tough on ideas and kind to each other, that focus on the possible and the positive, and how all will participate. Then we ask people to answer a question, something like this: What are your ideas for making this project work for your community? We invite everyone to think in silence and then share their best idea.

Here is where the facilitator needs to be fierce, that is, bold and utterly dedicated to the integrity of the process, to ensure that people offer their ideas succinctly. We write all the ideas on a flip chart, capturing each in just a few words. If we have 50 minutes and there are 80 people at the meeting, there are about 40 seconds to hear and capture each idea. After we hear from everyone once, we go around and collect the remaining ideas. This leaves even less time for each person. This is very hard for some who find it necessary to establish the context (or perhaps their importance) before they offer an idea.

The first person may say: "I am a biologist and my wife and I have lived here for forty years, and I've been studying the importance of trees for the cities. Our city is lagging behind other cities in the percentage of canopy needed. I think that this project needs to address this issue. I've been a member of a study group to collect data and will present our recommendations to the city council." This person just took 40 seconds without spelling out their idea.

I say: "Do you propose that we plant many trees on this site?"

If the answer is "Yes," we write down three words: "plant many trees." The person's background and knowledge are invaluable. But the community meeting, where the goal is to understand all the facets and possibilities, is not the place to explain them.

I would then suggest to the second person to jump directly to their idea without prefacing it. Slowly, we are able to establish a rhythm of rapid ideas that, like color points in a pointillist painting, create a larger image of the project.

All communities struggle with how to include those who are traditionally less likely to participate. If meetings are too technical and lengthy, those less accustomed to public meetings will feel lost and less likely to engage in the future. Every community has individuals with discretionary time and energy who are willing to spend many meetings pursuing their agenda. They will outlast others with less available time. If we are committed to engaging all sectors of the community, community processes should only last a few meetings. And respecting time is the key to such success.

Roles and Responsibilities

To have community meetings with meaning, all of the participants/partners must understand their roles and responsibilities.

Sponsors' task: The sponsors of community engagement can be government agencies, but also non-profits and businesses. They must explain their projects with clarity, trust in people's insights and take input seriously, and practice transparency. In my experience, agencies often are undecided about whether to welcome the public to join the decision-making process. A member of one government agency told me: "Community input doesn't help us create a better project. Why ask for input if all we get are complaints, resistance to change, and the 'government is the enemy' attitude? I wish the community would get out of our way so we can do our work." It is no wonder that organizers approach community meetings with caution.

Many agencies have no consistent procedures for community engagement. One staff member may only want to inform, while another wants to engage. This inconsistency contributes to the confusion. Not only may agency members have different styles, but various city departments may develop different methods, further confusing the situation. If we are to improve collaborative democracy, governments will need to become consistent and create procedures that are user-friendly, that respect input and take it seriously, and explain projects with clarity and transparency. It is better to have no community meeting than token ones where no one learns anything new.

Community members' task: The second partner is the community. Their role is to put aside their anger and shift to finding solutions that solve many problems at the same time. The community's job is to define a working vision of the future and come up with ideas for how a specific project leads to that vision. A vision is much more than an opinion and much more profound than personal likes/dislikes. It is not what one person or group wants to see, but what is the right thing to happen. It requires all participants to do two tasks: to present ideas and insights, and listen to the ideas of others with equal vigor and commitment. Only then can we be creative together. And creativity thrives in environments free of negativity, complaining, blaming, and reaction. A vision can never be a list of things we do not like or that we fear.

In the next pages, I will discuss ground rules to assist community members to be constructive and collaborative.

Professional consultants' task: The third group is professional consultants—designers, artists, planners, engineers, and the like—who now must become servant leaders. They need to put their egos aside to build upon the community's ideas. They help to realize, not displace, the community's vision. They must use their expertise to translate a collection of different ideas and possibilities

presented by the residents into a compelling proposal.
It doesn't mean that they must incorporate all ideas.
Designing is a lot like making maple syrup where you start
with 40 gallons of sap to create one gallon of syrup. The
design is any process that condenses the community's ideas
into the limits of space, time, and resources. This applies
equally to the shaping of cities, buildings, and open spaces,
and to events and programs. For design to work, it needs
to be powerful in its simplicity. It is not just a collection
of every idea. The consultants present the results of their
work to the community, explain how the community's
ideas live in that work, and explain the reasons why
specific ideas were not incorporated. This clear
communication increases the trust between community
members and consultants.

Facilitators' task: The crucial fourth partner is
the facilitator. Our responsibility is to be neutral. Being
neutral does not mean being passive. I chose the term
"fierce facilitation" because it requires powerful and
relentless commitment to the integrity of the process
while upholding a neutrality that allows for everyone's
participation. When facilitators betray even the tiniest
agenda or preference, they lose their credibility.

Facilitators' work with the sponsors and consultants
to ensure clarity in presenting the project, remove all
possible obstacles to creativity, ask the right questions,
involve everyone, encourage participants to learn from
each other, and explain where the process will lead next.
In short, facilitators do whatever it takes to maintain an
environment encouraging to fresh thinking and enhanced
by respect, trust, and creativity. We need to be fierce
because we will encounter the grandstanders, naysayers,
curmudgeons, and conspiracy theorists who show up

consistently to dominate and derail the proceedings. The core task is to balance inclusiveness and decisiveness, a narrow field where excellence and participation coexist. We help the consultants to respect and build upon the community's imagination while guiding community members to avoid micro-managing the design decisions.

Facilitators create an atmosphere where different insights contribute to, rather than extinguish, each other. We encourage all participants to take the ideas of others seriously. This increases the chances that the project will work for business and for the environment, that it will promote health and equity and will work for children. It is fantastic when it is also beautiful.

When I prepare for an upcoming community meeting, I actually visualize a field of discovery, an empty space in the center of the room. It is a space where ideas are exchanged. And I see my role to fiercely protect this field from invasion or annexation by any single user, ideology, mindset, or worldview.

I notice that those in positions of authority and leadership tend to be the most confident, often offering their views with firmness and without hesitation. Then I notice the quieter, more hesitant voices. Compared to their confident neighbors, they come across as tentative, maybe indecisive. Because they are not specialists, they think about a problem with directness and innocence, with fewer preconceptions. They can be better explorers. Sometimes I find their insights to be the most promising and exciting. I also notice that they are routinely ignored. Once I became aware of this, I began urging all to agree that it is okay to explore unconventional approaches because every new project is unique and requires fresh solutions. I ask people to pay equal attention to the quieter voices of people who may offer small "aha" moments, and who are able to connect the different ideas that people propose. Creativity flourishes in those moments.

When everyone steps up, extraordinary results are possible. In a brief time—and these days, people's discretionary time for such activities is rare and precious—people can create not only a shared vision but also develop steps to realize it. Action connected to a meaningful concept is compelling and enjoyable. The most significant benefit of this approach is the sense of ownership from all involved, resulting in pride that leads to stronger stewardship. The most satisfying part is that, when it all falls into place, participants experience civic joy. What a concept!

Part 2: Ground Rules for Community Collaboration

Through 30 years of leading public processes, we've learned the ground rules that enhance collaborative democracy. We share these guidelines with all involved with the project. They are the necessary conditions for collaboration. To Pomegranate Center they are indispensable in helping the participants elevate their expectations, generating creative, forward-looking results.

We witnessed how easily meetings can meander unproductively or become dominated by a few individuals while the majority remains silent and eventually unengaged. To counteract these tendencies, we ask all to agree to a set of ground rules. With the help of these rules, we accomplish more in less time.

When we ask participants if they agree to the ground rules, they generally say yes. For most it is acceptable. On rare occasions I need to clarify why this is essential. But this does not immediately change their attitudes. Their old habits will soon take over. This is where the facilitator's fierceness is needed, protecting the ground rules as unintentional (and sometimes intentional) violations occur. The key is not to get into battles with offending participants but to focus on the integrity of the process. So, when someone goes on and on, I say something like this: "We've agreed that everyone will have a chance to speak at this meeting, and I need to ask you for your idea and to bring your comment to a close so we can hear from others." Or when a person focuses exclusively on what they object to: "We've all agreed to focus on solutions. We understand what you dislike, but please share what you propose instead."

Sometimes a participant feels challenged. A few have walked out, offended. Every now and then a participant suggests that I go back to my communist country of origin. Who am I to suggest how democracy should work?

We use the ground rules in consultation with the partners who know the local culture much better than we do. They forewarn us about individuals who are likely to disrupt the meeting. "Nancy is going to bring up garbage in the park, as she always does," for example. So, we draft an occasion-specific ground rule to stay on topic of the meeting, allowing the facilitator to say: "Garbage in the park is for another meeting, but not this one." Or we are told that "Alfred will interrupt and speak over others," so we add a ground rule, "One conversation at a time."

The ground rule principles are:

- **Be tough on ideas and gentle on people:** Do not vilify the person, but examine the idea itself.
- **Assume that together we know more:** This ground rule is necessary to shift the conversation away from convincing others to consulting with others to discover the optimal idea.
- **Commit to finding common solutions with multiple uses:** The best ideas solve more than one problem at a time.
- **Propose something better:** It is okay to

identify the problems, but the focus should move to the solution.

- **Share air time. Everyone participates:** This is essential for giving the quieter voices the chance to be heard while keeping the more persistent voices in check. The result is that more people will feel the ownership of the decisions and will support their implementation in the future.

- **Listen and try to understand others' assumptions and views:** This is hard. We encourage listening as an active tool for discovery, rather than a passive period before speaking. Learn to see differences as assets.

- **Respect those with whom you disagree:** This is just basic civility. We offer seats to older people on the bus whether we like them or not. We should offer our ideas and our openness to others whether we like them or not.

- **Keep in mind the highest good for the community:** We ask people to stretch themselves beyond their immediate concerns and also serve future generations.

- **Maintain a balance between the mind and heart, knowledge and intuition, expertise and passion:** All contributions are welcome. Some people are comfortable speaking in broad principles and values, others in specific activities or objects.

- **Reject the culture and tactics of blame:** This is important in situations where negativity has become an accepted habit.

- **Confront internal contradictions. Practice compassion toward those who, like yourself, unwittingly contribute to the problems they wish to solve:** If we are upset by traffic but don't look for ways to reduce our car trips, then we are perpetuating a problem that we're unwilling to help solve.

We do not use all these ground rules at every meeting. We learn in advance which ones to select (or invent new ones) to defuse unproductive local habits.

What Does Success Look Like?

We consider it a great success when participants take charge of adherence to the agreements. We are delighted when a community member says, "Wait a minute. I thought we agreed not to blame each other." Or, "I know what you don't want, but I still don't know what you do want." Or even, "I'm willing to give up some of my ideas so that we can all gain something." We know we are on the right track when a participant says, "I can see how your proposal meets the functional needs, but if slightly modified, it can also meet environmental needs. What if we…?"

Once, a disgruntled meeting participant said to me that he did not need ground rules, even suggesting they were an insult. I was ready to respond when another person spoke up: "Hmm, Arthur (not his real name), it is because of people like you that we need them. You always talk too long and don't listen." It was a sweet moment, and Arthur turned into a model citizen for the rest of the meeting.

I have often seen a participant intervene in a neighbor's blaming tirade: "Hey, I know you are angry. But all the rest of us want to solve the problem at hand. Please offer something or pass."

The facilitator's job is to assure a fair and open discussion, to nudge the group toward shared solutions, and to end on time.

We have learned that successful facilitation is part artform, part science. Facilitation science is about managing space and time and providing a transparent and precise process that encourages people to be constructive with each other. The art is evident when the facilitator is able to build trust by balancing individual and group needs. Good facilitators have a kind of natural authority that lets them remain centered in the face of possible anger and hostility. They must be quick on their feet, able to listen, provide feedback and synthesize complex ideas in the midst of serious discourse and help people arrive at a conclusion together.

Because each person is smart in some areas yet blessedly foolish in others, it makes sense to ask what others see and think, to trade ideas and patch the holes in each other's awareness, and together construct solutions that are greater than any one individual's knowledge.

When it comes to community—the maddening but enriching mix of cultures, ideologies, sensibilities, and tastes—the profound truth is that together we always know more. Facilitation is the sacred work of tending to the field of discovery where participatory democracy can breathe. And, yes, it takes courage and fierceness.

I've worked long and hard to learn how to protect the ground rules rather than wrestle with people; to be firm yet respectful; to model the conduct I asked others to uphold; to master how to maintain my neutrality; and to balance firmness with gentleness. It takes practice.

And slowly, as we practice this new behavior, a new

habit is formed. In time, it becomes an accepted tradition. Conclusion: together we are capable of extraordinary achievements when we uphold agreed-upon ground rules.

Part 3: Ground Rules in Action

The following vignettes illustrate the breadth and variety of settings in which the Pomegranate Method has been implemented with success.

•

Together we know more

Our brains are complicated, brilliant instruments capable of great discoveries when we establish synapses among diverse parts. Communities can be similarly dazzling when we see each other as sources of knowledge rather than as enemies or irritating distractions. This attitude of generosity and largess makes it possible to connect the dots among different parts of our shared wisdom, uncovering new and exciting possibilities.

•

What's Next for a Decommissioned School?

A senior woman was angry and didn't like the new development being planned for her neighborhood:

"Do you have any ideas for how this project could work?"

"I oppose this project."

"On what grounds?"

"It will destroy things I care about."

"What things?"

45

"Views and old trees."

"Would you support this project if we find a way to protect the views and mature trees?"

"The developers will cut down every tree. I've seen it all."

"Our team wants to do the right thing. What would you have us do?"

"Protect the most important views. Save old trees."

"Thank you for proposing a solution."

Transit Solutions

When working with communities, I ask them at the beginning if they are prepared to make small changes in their lives. One town considered a proposal to have bus service connect different neighborhoods. However, when it came to adopting it into the planning goals, one of these same people said: "I like buses. But I don't like the thought of a bus stop next to my home."

Others chimed in with the same reluctance, citing fumes, strangers loitering, and noise. I was surprised that people ignored all the benefits: The bus stop just steps away is convenient when I bring groceries from the store, seeing children disembarking, or bumping into neighbors more regularly. It was an illustration of how fear blinds us from seeing new possibilities.

A woman offered a way out: "We can't have it both ways. If we want transit, we need to accept bus stations that will be close to some of our homes. I am okay with a station being in front of my home."

Incorporating a Long History

We heard from the tribal elders about the atrocities

of forced resettlement to make space for a mill and later industrial uses. We understood anger and hurt and the need for healing. The design that emerged from those conversations was equal parts art and healing. We heard ideas for what the project's elements should be, but mainly we heard slow healing should accompany the project.

It is the quiet people in the room, those who listen and observe, who often bring forth insights that ultimately make projects work. They are better able to see the value of many perspectives and find solutions that combine two or more proposals. We call on each person, one at a time. This allows the quieter and gentler people to have a say. This creates a "field" of many ideas that indicate people's care.

When we listen to all, we create for all, and we create a more vibrant, more meaningful, and better-owned future.

Affordable Housing

A long-time resident stated that her life had been steadily going downward.

"New people who did not even speak English are moving in, desiring affordable rental places. Why don't they work as hard as we did and buy their own houses? Any changes will only downgrade our neighborhood."

A new immigrant spoke: "I am so excited to live here. My job is nearby so I would love to have my home here. A small one is all I need." This was good for the first woman to hear.

She slowly softened her anger and talked about the unique treasures she wants to protect. Is there a way to make changes without destroying? This was good for the newcomers to hear. They started to understand and respect the community's history and its uniqueness. The project was better for it.

It is okay to have different opinions as long as they lead to deeper understanding. Respect allows this to happen.

Neighborhood Planning

A complainer can trigger an avalanche of reactions. Here is an undesirable scenario:

First participant: "This meeting is a sham. The council doesn't listen."

Second participant: "Yes, they completely ignored my ideas for flower pots at the street corners."

Third: "The City has already made plans. They are not interested in our ideas. They've never been."

Fourth: "Yes, and...."

Before we know it, complaining and blaming take over. It doesn't help anyone, and it leaves a bitter taste for all.

Here is a more positive scenario:

"This meeting is a sham. The council doesn't listen?"

Before anyone else has a chance to speak, I, as facilitator jump in: "I understand. Let's have a beer afterward. But right now, we are collecting ideas for the future. I would like to hear yours, and then those of everyone else. So what idea can you offer?"

"I have plenty of ideas that I shared many times before."

"Yes. But tonight, we want to hear all the ideas from everybody to see what solutions will emerge from the community's collective wisdom. What is your idea?"

"I have many."

"Just give me one." "Car-free streets like I've seen in Europe. I also...."

"Thank you. I will circle back to collect your remaining ideas later."

Benches for a Shelter

We learned that tribal elders needed seating. We heard that they wanted their traditional designs in the project. We also heard that the winds could be harsh, and that protection was required during storms. Three different ideas, each one presented by a different person. One person suggested that we use the face of each bench for art. What if we also made benches that could stack and form a buffer against the winds and rain? We ended with benches that could stack five high, and when assembled in a recommended order, displayed traditional artworks. Without the commitment to find a common solution, we would have ended up with three different ideas.

Thinking on Behalf of all

A local agency identified five possible sites for a project. We called a meeting for people from all five neighborhoods. We showed images and conditions of each space, and then asked everyone the same question: Where would our project offer the highest service and usefulness? During the first round of responses, every group promoted their own neighborhood's site. We made no progress.

After the break, I asked them to shift: What is best for the city? Then a small miracle happened. A woman from an affluent neighborhood said that she changed her mind: Another community needed the project more. She presented several reasons. Her position opened a floodgate for others to follow with ideas for how other neighborhoods could best benefit from the proposed project. In a short time, the group agreed to focus their collective energies on the site of the least affluent neighborhood.

Afterward, she told me that when I prompted her to

think more broadly, she looked at the entire city, and it became evident that her neighborhood's need paled in comparison with the lack of amenities in the less affluent neighborhood. In her mind, she visited all the sites and, when she lined them all together, it became clear: "We should help the least-affluent neighborhood. They need it the most, and the rest of us will learn from their efforts so we can make similar projects in our neighborhoods in the future."

Children's Park

One group of recent Americans proposed to surround a park with barbed wire and, if the funds allowed, electrify it. In their experience, this was the only image for safety. What did others think? Lights at night, hedges instead of fences, benches for parents to always see their children, beautiful flowers. It continued like this for a while. Then the mother who initially proposed the wires said: "Wires are not right for children. We need beauty. Dostoyevsky said that beauty will save the world. Let's make something beautiful, and our children will be safe."

Watershed Restoration

"If salmon are indeed in trouble, how come we can buy cat food with salmon in it?" asked a participant discussing watershed health. In response, the county biologist corrected her: "The salmon in cat food is not from the local species that is suffering and could disappear. The biologist added that property owners, therefore, could develop new practices: Create buffer zones, slow down the water. Let's work together to protect your watershed."

The next person completely ignored what the biologist had said and went on to repeat the same inaccurate, but predetermined, talking point. I gently reminded them that we had agreed to be willing to change our minds, and I was curious to hear their new ideas that would build upon, rather than ignore, the views of others. In response, some huffed and puffed and were offended by my ground rule. But most were able to work with it, and the future meetings became more constructive and useful.

All Contributions Count

We always have individuals who are fond of proposing values and broad concepts, such as safety, beauty, health, or justice. On the other extreme are people who narrow their comments to very particular ideas: a six-foot fence, a mosaic celebrating orca whales, motion-detecting lights, etc. Another group is comfortable describing activities: walking, dancing, eating, etc.

If we're not careful, we may disregard others' ideas because their emphasis is different from our own. Some would argue that walking and health are two different ideas when in fact they promote the same spirit. Walking is one of the activities that support health. It is not the only one, but it serves as a specific illustration of how we can promote health.

Trees in the City

I was at a meeting once discussing the importance of urban trees. Unexpectedly, two different environmental themes emerged. First, plant many trees to provide shade and absorb carbon. Second, don't plant trees that block sunlight from reaching our solar panels. At first, the two ideas appeared to conflict. Then one person said that perhaps taller buildings could become the prime spaces for solar panels. From that moment on we all started to think about how this win–win solution could happen, resulting in many more productive ideas. Commonly supported solutions emerged. It ended up being a joyful experience.

Part 4: Things Anyone can do to Strengthen Everyday Democracy

If I want to become a virtuoso pianist, I have to practice. The same applies to becoming a community builder and a collaboration wizard. It doesn't happen automatically. Here are some ways to start—some simple, and others, I admit, challenging. The good news is that almost everything we do gives us an opportunity to engage in community-minded behavior. With practice, we'll find it becomes an increasingly large part of our everyday life. Let's give it a try.

Clarify Your Image of the Future

We have a choice: Direct the change or complain about it. Taking charge means articulating a vision of how the future ought to be. We should start with our hunches and intuitions, or let our indignation guide us. How could our community and society work better? We should take a hard look at our assumptions, prejudices, and blind spots. Train an internal microscope on our impulses and ask, "Do these represent my highest and best values?" Perhaps they are vestiges of childhood misunderstandings, outmoded cultural views, or merely old ideas we've never bothered to question. I should discard the ideas that serve neither the community nor me. This will give me a new sense of purpose and direction.

A shared image of the future serves the same purpose for the society as the picture on the jigsaw puzzle box does for the family putting it together. Imagine what pandemonium would happen if people tried to assemble the puzzle without a guiding image. We would force pieces into each other whether they fit or not.

The same thing is happening in our society. We are jamming together different agendas that will not link because they are informed by different imaginations.

The great work that lies ahead is to develop a shared image of the future. And this can only happen if we engage honestly and courageously with each other.

Get Involved in the Life of Your Community

We should vote. We should also attend meetings where new developments are discussed. We should bring our best selves to those meetings, and resist the temptation to instantly take sides, deride other's ideas, or become disrespectful. At first, we should listen and learn. Then we should propose solutions that link our thoughts with those of others and exhibit the most public and creative conduct. We should strive to do our part of creating a learning environment where people become wiser together. Improvise on Pomegranate Center's ground rules and develop your own list that will guide you in your conduct.

Walk the Tightrope

Creativity is fostered by the tension between the possible and the real. The more ambitious your image of the future, the higher the need for balance. Resist the temptation to choose between becoming a realist or an idealist. When you walk in balance, you are both focused on the task AND open to new ideas and approaches.

Generate Passion for Someone Else's Passion

It's easy to believe that we have all the answers. But remember, no matter how acute our vision, we see only part of the picture. Studying what it's like to stand in someone else's shoes brings valuable new perspectives.

Pledge Allegiance to Your Community

First to your community of place, second to your community of interest. Geography defines a place, and this often includes people with whom we have little in common except physical proximity. Our future depends on finding ways to collaborate with people who have divergent viewpoints. Healthy communities transform differences among people into gifts.

Invite "Them" to Your Meeting

It can be comforting and familiar to imagine it's "us" against "them." But it can also be destructive. Often "they" have insights that can help us better understand the problem and, as a result, discover creative solutions that might otherwise stay hidden. Learn to value the ideas of the diverse people around you. This is the foundation of a healthy community.

The most interesting, essential discoveries can happen in the spaces between interests, disciplines, and ideologies. In order to uncover new solutions, step outside of your comfort zone.

Consider Your Own Internal Contradictions First-- Don't Play the Blame Game

Insisting the problem is someone else's fault conveniently absolves us from doing our part. We can't come up with solutions by waiting for others to change THEIR behavior—especially when OUR behavior is a piece of the problem. Did I just fly across the world to attend an environmental conference? Did I just drive solo to a meeting to complain about traffic? Take a moment to smile at the irony of our routines. Then view your actions with the same compassion and understanding that your fellow community members deserve when you notice that they, too, unwittingly add to the problems they are demanding everyone else should solve.

The humility that arises when we admit we're part of the problem is fertile ground for collaborating to devise fresh solutions. Let's assume we've all had a hand in creating the problem; now let's join hands to come up with a solution.

Be a Mentor for Those who are Less Involved

Every community looks to a small, overworked group of leaders and expects them to "figure it out" for the rest of us. They attend the meetings and take on formidable piles of work, while others stand by in silence—until it's time to complain. If you've been sitting on the sidelines complaining about local conditions to friends and family, approach a community leader you admire and ask them to be your mentor. If you are a leader, pull a couple of people off the "bench" and offer to mentor them—especially if they've been complaining.

Have Opponents, not Enemies

We challenge and engage opponents. We shoot down enemies. There will always be people we want to exclude: developers, environmentalists, new immigrants, youth-at-risk, government regulators, etc. Instead, invite yourself to their meetings and encourage them to attend yours. This simple practice builds bridges for a better future.

Promote the Architecture of Encounter

Unintentional interactions happen in intentional places: public plazas, main streets, churches, parks, stores, pubs, coffee houses, farmers' markets, schools, and theaters. After seeing a stranger five times, we may nod. After ten such nods, maybe we say, "hello." Ten "hellos" may lead to a casual conversation. A sense of community can spring up when we spontaneously bump into people we don't know. It can't happen when we hide in gated communities and home theaters to avoid random encounters with "strangers." Public places can be fascinating classrooms that teach us how to be neighbors. Knowing our neighbors helps us to imagine the future together, and it sets the stage for making it into reality.

Whatever we do, let's Make it Beautiful

Read Miss Rumphius, my family's favorite children's book.

Functionality without artistry, beauty, or even mystery deprives our souls of vital nourishment. When beauty is baked into our work, more people use our malls, streets, bridges, and town squares and they do it with more enthusiasm, civility, and respect. Infrastructure then becomes a source of local identity and pride.

Dare to Build Cathedrals

Most medieval craftsmen who labored to build great cathedrals didn't live long enough to see the results of their labor. Nevertheless, they invested their sweat equity in a vision of a place where the sacred became tangible.

They understood they were doing more than laying down stones—they aimed toward a physical expression of their highest ideals. With each stone, they paid homage to their faith in the future—a future they would not live to see. We honor that tradition by building our surroundings with future generations in mind rather than bowing only to the demands of the next fiscal year. We, too, can build communities as expressions of our highest ideals. Our children's grandchildren's lives depend on it.

Thanks

Visual art comes naturally to me. Even composing songs, as I did in my youth, was relatively effortless. Crafting sentences in my second language is harder work for me. I've always written to myself as homework for training and talks.

Writing for others is hard work. Now I needed to make sense to those who are not me. I would read what I wrote each day and think to myself: Who is this idiot? So, in a typical Pomegranate fashion, I turned for help to my colleagues and friends. I asked them to read through my drafts and guide me toward improvements. Their contributions were immense.

Lynn Parker, a Board alumnus, who was the first who encouraged me to write and helped me get started;

Warren Wilson for being a fierce editor and guide over the last few drafts;

Pomegranate Center board members: Dawn Bushnaq and Joe Barrett, who read early drafts and urged me forward;

Paul Eichen, Grace Mazur, and my wife Kathi, who offered the right mix of brutal honesty and encouragement;

Allison Wilson, Ray Kelleher, Katya Matanovič, Liz St.Andre and Kait Heacock for edits over the years, some of which live in this handbook.

All these individuals bravely plowed through my ramblings and helped me become more focused.

I have borrowed portions of this handbook from my previous writings, published over the years.

This handbook was made possible through grants from the Szekely Family Foundation and the San Diego Foundation.

Thank you!

About Pomegranate Center

Pomegranate Center trains individuals and agencies in effective community engagement based on collaborative principles. Milenko Matanovic founded the non-profit in 1986, and has spent over three decades on the ground exploring the realities of community building, participatory democracy, civility, and creativity. The Center's most notable past projects are the 60+ gathering places built with communities around the Pacific Northwest and California, with select projects in other states and countries. Pomegranate Center now focuses on promoting collaborative practices by:

- conducting training for government and non-profit agencies, design professionals, and community builders;
- consulting with organizations interested in improving their community-building capacity;
- designing and facilitating public processes;
- developing educational materials; and
- presenting Pomegranate Center's findings at conferences and gatherings

To learn more, visit us at pomegranatecenter.org or email info@pomegranate.org

About the Author

Milenko is a community builder, artist and social innovator who has spent over three decades exploring the art of creative collaboration. He started the non-profit Pomegranate Center in 1986 after leaving a successful art career. His work has been exhibited internationally, including the 2017 Biennale of Venice.

As the founder of Pomegranate Center, he has worked with many neighborhoods around the country and abroad. Milenko has collaborated with numerous communities to build more than 60 gathering places. He helped develop community-owned plans for parks, town centers, streets, and trails and trained hundreds of leaders in the Pomegranate Center method of community building. He teaches that, when it comes to society, together we always know more and that empowering communities is the most efficient, foundational way to improve society.

Milenko now focuses on education. He's a popular speaker and consults with governments and nonprofits on community engagement, collaboration, and creative placemaking. He is working on additional handbooks to explore the diverse aspects of creativity, collaboration, and fierce facilitation.

47126470R00044

Made in the USA
San Bernardino, CA
10 August 2019